Renovating Hotel Bathrooms: Get the Spa-Like Bath Your Guests Want at a Fraction of the Cost and in Half the Time

An Interview with Orlando P. Salazar

Table of Contents

Forward

The following interview took place in May 2016 with Orlando P. Salazar. During this interview we discussed:

- Orlando's extensive professional experience in hotel bath renovations,
- The role of bathrooms in hotel reviews
- The impact of reviews on hotel revenue
- The importance of timely renovations and how renovations – particularly in the bath area – can positively impact revenue
- Challenges and pre-planning for renovation
- And an in-depth understanding of refinishing, and how it can shorten the renovation cycle, thus positively impacting hotel revenues and staff productivity.

Successful hotel renovations can create a wealth of opportunity, guest engagement, and publicity. Hotel bath expert Orlando Salazar shares how to navigate this challenging landscape to ensure a successful remodel.

Introduction

Christina McCale (host): Hi everyone and welcome to
Revitalizing Your Hotel Bathrooms. Today's interview is
sponsored by hoteltubspro.com helping property managers,
owners or operations managers with how to get the luxurious
bathrooms, you'll get one at a fraction of the cost and in less
than half the time. Check out hoteltubspro.com for more.

Today we're talking about how to get the luxurious
bathrooms you want for your hotel or apartment complex at
a fraction of the cost and in half the time. My name is
Christina McCale and today I'm talking with bathroom and
renovation expert Orlando P. Salazar about how every
property manager, owner or operations manager can get
started on the right track with renovating their hotel
bathrooms and obtaining the best results and of course doing
it affordably too. Orlando, thank you again for joining us on
this live interview.

Orlando Salazar (guest/industry expert): Hey Christina, how
are you? You're welcome.

Christina: Let's just jump right in. First tell us a bit about
your background and the experience that you have in the
field of bathroom renovations, just so that the property
managers or the owners of hotels or operations managers in
our audience can understand who you are and where you're
coming from and how you can relate to where they're at in
their jobs.

Orlando: Great, no problem. I came here from Chile, South
America back in 1976 that was a long time ago, and I had
just come out of high school. When I was 17, I took one year
of English because I knew I was coming to the States after
my dad and I wanted to be off to a good start. And hey, I was
fascinated with the idea of coming to live in America! But my
dad didn't let me waste any time. I went to work with him to
help out bring the rest of the family to the States.

I started spray painting wood cabinets, where my dad used to work as a carpenter. Then fast forward to '79, I took a job with a bathtub refinishing company. I traveled all over the New York area, met all kinds of people and saw every kind of bathroom problem imaginable; the good, the bad, the ugly for sure.

Seven years after that in August '86, I took the plunge and began building a family business. I set out to make a unique bathroom repair service better and a real money saver for consumers. The strategy was to provide faster and much better service than Long Islander's were getting at the time, plus a longer lasting job.

Christina: Wow, so you have been refinishing bathrooms for almost 40 years, you're going to have some incredible experience.

Orlando: Yes, I'm going on 37 years right now.

Christina: That's incredible, you're going to have some incredible experiences I know our listeners and our readers are going to benefit from. Tell us a little bit more about yourself in terms of background and education and how you really learned bathroom refinishing?

Orlando: My refinishing roots go back 37 years ago to 1979 in a company called New Glaze Industries, now long gone. My skills took me to other re-glazing companies that never grew.

Then in August '86, like I said, Bathtub Doctor was found which went from a basement startup to a highly recognized team, serving thousands of residential home owners, apartments, general contractors, architects, real estate management companies, government facilities, hotels, hospitals, restaurants et cetera, here in the Nassau and Suffolk counties [Long Island, New York] and the greater New York metropolitan area.

Christina: That's a really broad background of people you've been serving for a really long time. Is there any formal education or training in the bathroom renovation industry or is it pretty much been all hands-on, on the job kind of training?

Orlando: Not really, Christina, but I studied photography, I got a certificate in commercial photography in the early 80s. I believe that went a long way to help me develop an eye for visual appearance, the use of color, light and texture.

The rest was all the experience of 30 years on the job training with thousands of hotel rooms, apartments and commercial facilities, refinished and all types of remodeling as well. I was self-taught, I went to workshops, online courses, you name it. I've done my share of self-study.

Christina: That's an incredible amount of work to have done all of that. What have your experiences taught you that help you understand what hotel or property managers go through and the considerations that they have to think through before they embark on a renovation?

Orlando: Great question. I like to answer that with a comparison, very typical from the home remodel industry because I've been doing residential refinishing and remodeling as well. I've seen, when you're first looking at a house, the first rooms you look at are the bathrooms and kitchens. These usually either make or break the sale, or are subject to negotiations. My point is, if you're thinking about renovating hotel rooms, the bathrooms are key and a priority. Not so much the kitchens, most hotel rooms don't have kitchens. Most guests want to see a nice, clean and bright bathroom, bathtub or shower or toilet et cetera.

Most demanding guests want the home-away-from-home experience or better. They are up to date with the latest bath designs, they expect the trendy looks, the modern amenities. After all, they booked the room online because they saw what they liked. If they don't see that when they get there, they

usually ask for another room or worse the bad review is
already in the making.

The Role of Bathrooms in Hotel Reviews & Revenue

Christina: Reviews are so vital to the hotel industry, in fact, a Trust You survey was done back in 2014 and it seemed that the actual location, service and the quality of the rooms were the most important attributes that were mentioned more than anything else in their reviews. In terms of issues about bathrooms, oh my goodness, such as their cleanliness and their size, those characteristics were imperative to the reviewers. Given that negative reviews were 2.24, so two and a quarter times more likely than positive wants to include some kind of comment about the bathroom.

Orlando: This is not unknown Christina. As a matter of fact, in the last few hotels I've been working in, they had this poster out in housekeeping departments, of the most important things the housekeepers need to keep in mind when cleaning up rooms, [and a lot of it was about] bathrooms, bathrooms, bathrooms, bathrooms.

Christina: Oh my goodness.

Orlando: Items in the bathroom: you can imagine what goes on in there. Cleaning the shower, cleaning the bath... if there is a problem, report it, make a note for housekeeping or for engineering. All these things are there as priorities on the walls, at the housekeeping departments, but they're being ignored every day. How many times do you go into a hotel and you see the bathroom is in kind of bad shape.

Christina: It's good that the hotel industry recognizes that and so they're really trying to reinforce [the importance of clean rooms – especially baths] that with their staff.

I think it's safe to say that while a good review might not necessarily include comments about the hotel bath, if our listeners are really trying to focus on making sure that they check those things off that can create the opportunity for a bad review, man, hotel baths are right up there in the big three that contribute to bad hotel bath reviews.

What makes this even more important and I know you know this, a recent survey was conducted by Search Engine Land and found that 88% of people now trust online reviews as much as personal recommendations.

Positive reviews on review websites, like TripAdvisor, can be extremely beneficial for our hotel customers. According to hospitalityandresourcetools.com, one star, just a one star increase in your online average review rating can increase your hotel's income by 9%. Tell me there isn't a hotel operations manager or a hotel general manager out there who wouldn't love to try to increase their operations or their revenue by 9%!

Then, in addition to that, 360Commerce found that revenues rose by 56% for hotels that consistently generate good online reviews.

Orlando you've been into this business a long time, what's your take one these findings?

Orlando: I find it that these statements are true because I see it every day. If you make a small little bit of change throughout the hotel as far as cleaning, maintaining, keeping those rooms upgraded, so people are happy, they move on, that makes a big difference.

If you are complicating things, and stop [improving], rip out things, and make major renovations, you better have your plan together. Otherwise [things aren't going to turn out the way you want them to.] It's not going to work and it's not going to look pretty before you start making progress.

The Boom in Hotel Renovation

Christina: Let's fast forward to 2016.

It's 2016 and depending on who you talk to, we're seeing an economic recovery, which, at least if you look at the trade press these days, seems to have launched a whole lot of companies, hotels, et cetera into some major renovation projects. I'm thinking of like The Peninsula Hotel that just finished up a 37 million dollar renovation of like 90% of its suites, the Four Seasons with its Lanai property in Hawaii.

Why is now really the time to start considering renovating?

Orlando: Well, we're already into spring, [it's time for] clean up days and more hotels are getting ready for their busy summer season, if they haven't already started.

You don't want to be left out especially with those bathrooms "in a deferred maintenance status." You want to set yourself up for a successful season, clean up house, have happy guests and get great reviews.

Brands are in full remodel/renovation mode right now, and management must keep up in order to be competitive: attract demanding guests, [who are also] the most profitable type of guest, by the way.

If you feel you have missed the deadline to do something about those rooms, you can still upgrade and complete the project before the busiest time of the year is here. Most refinishing and live remodel will take days, not months to do.

By the time we complete your project, you will have nothing to be envious about with your competitors. We'll keep your costs under control, and [soon you'll] be all lined up for a profitable 2016. You can start doing something about it, before you think it's too late – or you can put it off until next year or who knows when.

Christina: That's a really good point, I really hope our listeners and our readers caught what you just said.

It doesn't have to take months and months and months of work, it really can be done [in a short amount of time]. At least the types or renovations you're talking about, which can be high impact renovations, and they can be done in a very short amount of time.

Orlando: Yes. There are ways to do big time renovations that requires a lot of planning, budget, and months and months in the making. That's probably something that is in the works for a five year, eight-year period.

That may not be what you're thinking now, but a lot can be accomplished by downsizing and doing what needs to be done – maybe requiring a lot more time and a lot more money to do.

You can accomplish similar results doing the project that really needs to be done as fast, which is the most important part of the hotel room, which is the bathroom.

Christina: It reminds me of that old saying that I think my grandmother used to say always, which was, "A stitch in time saves nine." If you just do those little things, they may seem like little things but if you do them when they're needed, it can have big results and big impact over time.

Where do you see the beginner property manager or a hotel owner, or an operations manager wasting a lot of time when planning or managing their bathroom renovations?

Orlando: I think primarily new managers, [tend] to put priority on sales and bookings, and at the same time overlook different maintenance issues, putting the renovation on hold until room occupancy drops which sometimes doesn't come, so they fail to plan.

Again, a bathroom remodel involves new plumbing, fixtures, new tubs or showers – it's a major undertaking. We're talking millions of dollars for a few hundred rooms.

If you, as a general manager, are struggling to get a budget approval, you're in for a surprise. It could take years – actually about eight, or five to eight years rather on average – for an approved renovation budget. It takes a while.

Christina: Boy, that reminded me of ... How does the saying go? "If you fail to plan, you plan to fail."

Orlando: It's very true.

Christina: You really have to be on top of it. Sounds like what you're saying, operations managers and general managers have to be on top of, not just keeping an eye on the hotel bookings but also on what's that clock of passage of time in terms of, when was the last time they did their last renovation. How is their hotel holding up in terms of wear and tear?

They need to keep an eye on both aspects of their business, not just hotel bookings although I'm sure that's an important part, it's not the only part.

Orlando: Usually management is under pressure to perform. They have sales quotas. They have goals to meet. They have bonuses in mind, all the time. Especially when the Quarters end is coming around, they want to see numbers. Management wants to see reports, bookings. They want to see how many people are coming in next 30 days? 60 days? 90 days? What is ahead of us? Is there a short on that?

The first thing they're going to sacrifice is whether a room needs to be put off – out of service – so they can do repairs. They're going to book the room, so they can get the rate in, so they can get paid, so they can collect money. That seems to be priority for that type of management.

Christina: That seems awfully shortsighted though in some ways, because it seems like, and I know this is a little of a side topic here, but it seems like that's a little shortsighted.

You should be keeping an eye also on how your hotel looks, especially in this environment of where everybody is so ready to go jump on Google and not only Google a hotel and see what the reviews are like, but also they go write a negative review. It just seems like that would be very shortsighted.

Orlando: Yes, there's a very close balance of performance, sales and keeping up with maintenance at the same time.

There is a struggle between housekeeping and the sales department, constantly, I find. We can't get into a room a lot of time because the room was scheduled for maintenance [but then is later booked for guest occupancy]. It's not because they forgot, it's because they just wanted to sell the room.

Most hotels are computerized and they have electronic management systems. They can just click a button, and the room is out service. Or they can click a button and the room is reserved.

Christina: It's a delicate balance between doing the maintenance as you go versus, "I really want to make that fill room/make that sale right now."

Orlando: It's like everything else. I have to assume in other industries are the same way, they take the equipment out service when somebody needs to use the equipment to make money with it and you can't make money without the equipment. It's what comes first. This points to priority.

Christina: In a lot of ways, I think we all probably are. That's probably just human nature. [For example] you hear something with your car and, [you think] "Oh it can't be that bad, it's not that bad," and then you don't hear this sound for a couple of days and the next thing you know you're replacing a transmission. If, when you heard it that first time, you had just taken it into the mechanic, you might have saved yourself a thousand dollar repair.

Orlando: It's not any different. But the thing is, managers need to be understanding that, if you don't do the necessary small things like maintenance issues – like that's what we do, we do low end renovations compared to big time remodeling.

We can go in there and clean things up, make things looking clean, presentable, attractive, and also keep the room from degrading to the point that you need to rip it out and remodel completely. We can maintain things and keep them from deteriorating to the point that you need to really go ahead and you're just no turning back and you had to remodel.

Challenges and Pre-Planning for Renovations

Christina: Tell me, what are the biggest challenges for a property or an operations manager in planning or orchestrating a renovation?

Orlando: Two things, and I never get tired of repeating myself, it's all about time and money. How much is it going to cost me? When will it be done? How long will it take, so we can go back to booking those rooms again?

We help brands to stay competitive, by doing the project on time and on a much more attractive package than traditional remodeling can offer. Have a surge of bookings coming next month? It's easy, get those rooms done and ready in a weekend, believe it or not. It's all possible through refinishing, without the loss of revenues, the fuss, the noise, the dust, et cetera, and without the hustles of renovating or construction.

A Checklist of Questions
Christina: It sounds like the biggest issues that you're seeing property managers and operations manager space is that challenge of, "How do I get the renovations done in a timely manner, and on a budget, and get those rooms back as fast as I possibly can, so that I can start renting those rooms out, like yesterday?"

Orlando: Yes, managers should familiarize themselves with the renovation process also.

- Whether remodeling or refinishing, they should ask questions like,
- What are our options?
- Do we get renovation estimates?
- Do we scale down to the minimum or which contract to consider.
- If the basis for selecting the contractor is refinishing the bathrooms, what process will he be using?

- What is his scope of work?
- What's included in the scope of work? And are the must-haves included. What I really want, is_____. Is it included?
- What I don't want? Can I change that?

...All these questions, they should be asking.

Christina: That is a great checklist of questions that if you're a new property manager or if it's been a while since you've done a renovation, that's a really, really good list of questions for people to consider.

Step 1: The Room Audit
What's the first step for a property manager or an owner or an operations manager, what's the first step they need to take when considering taking on a remodeling project. What's step number one?

Orlando: Managers should think about getting estimates or a survey a project as to determine what needs to be done, what should be remodeled complete and what should be preserved or renewed?
A lot of times, plumbing and electrical systems are in good conditions, they should last maybe 25 years at least from new. Some rooms should be gut out, but most won't need to. Most existing tubs and showers can be refinished like new and some tubs would need to be removed to make room for a large shower or handicap room.

Christina: Let me repeat this partly. It sounds like you're saying one big favor that hotel property managers can do for themselves is, instead of saying, "Oh I'm just going to throw out all 200 bathrooms," they could go through room, by room, by room and really see which rooms are the problems. Which ones really have big problems, and which rooms could just get by for a while with maybe a little bit of tweaking here and there.

Orlando: Yes, depending on their engineering department, they should have a list of which rooms are updated rooms, which rooms that were never done before, rooms that were done halfway, and whatever.

Again, good record keeping will show that. A lot of times they don't have records or the last engineer is nowhere in sight, and maybe took the records with him or the computer lost the records, or whatever.

If they don't have that information, they have to obtain the list manually, they got to go room by room, check everything out and that's the only way to do it.

Christina: That's a really good point. Why is this such an important first step and what's the best way for them to take this step?

Orlando: Again, time and money and savings are at stake here. An engineering survey can be done in-house or by calling our toll free number; 877-882-3621. We can provide a full bathroom visual system inspection, and give you a report showing you our survey results of what needs to be addressed.

Christina: That's a great idea. Can you go into a little bit more detail about that?

Orlando: Sure. We look at:
- structurally sound walls and floors,
- water damage,
- moisture problems that might lead to mildew and rot,
- tiles and grout,
- shower doors,
- the caulking,
- lights,
- electrical outlets,
- switches,
- ventilating and air conditioning.

We check all of the above room, by room.

Christina: I bet that's really handy for an operations manager who's really trying to get a sense of how much has to be done, and how expensive is this renovation going to look.

Orlando: Actually it's cheaper that we do it for them, because we have a system – a checklist – that goes through the whole thing and then puts out the result and then gives them full report.

They don't have to take time off their schedule or they don't have to use their staff members to do that, which probably gets done maybe halfway, then it takes another week, then it takes maybe a month, or maybe it doesn't get done.

Christina: Got it. If somebody gets stuck at this point, how can they get unstuck?

Orlando: What I have found over the years, the reason managers run into problems is the lack of communication and synchronization of activities between their sales, housekeeping and engineering department.

A lot of times you cannot inspect and work in a room because it was not blocked out by housekeeping, or because engineering didn't send a memo to have it blocked and taken off the schedule. It comes down to how committed they are to see the project started and completed.

Step 2: What are your goals?
Christina: What is the next step then? Now that we've done the survey: we know what condition the rooms are in. What's the next step for the property manager to take when they're looking at planning this major renovation?

Orlando: Sure. Management needs to have clear goals and commitment to the renovation project. Without the goals in mind, there is no urgency or priority to move the project through the schedule.

Christina: Isn't that the truth, we always need a reason, a goal or a reason to put a priority on things in our lives, whether it's planning a renovation for a hotel or doing something for ourselves as simple as renovating our own homes or losing those 10 pounds or anything in life. We need to always have to have a reason to do it, why is this so important?

Orlando: Also let me add to that. If they expect to have – whatever the goal is for that year – $3 million, $5 million, $10 million [in sales], whatever the goal is, you have to have those [hotel guests] in.

Before you can collect the payments on those rooms, those rooms need to be usable. Guests need to be there, paying those weekly rates, whatever they are. Without those paying guests in there, those goals are not going to be met: they're not going to be achievable.

How do you get those room bookings? You got to keep people coming in.

If the people come in, they don't like what they see, they're not going to keep coming back or they're going to give bad reviews.

Those goals are going to be out of sight for that year if things work out that way (that guests get to a hotel and are disappointed in what they see). Renovations should be planned.

Christina: Setting goals: what is it that we want to accomplish and why is it that we want to accomplish. It's really important – before you even start thinking about renovation – to understand what those goals are.

Why is this is an important step again?

Orlando: It's important because you have to determine what we want to accomplish this year? How many rooms? What kind of percentage of occupancy we want to keep on a monthly basis if those rooms aren't up to speck.

If those rooms aren't up to the standards of today – standards like tiptop shape – those occupancy numbers are not going to be achievable. That means you're not going to have the bookings you planned. You're not going to have the people paying for those rooms, and those quarterly goals are not going to be achieved, and goals are not going to be achieved at the end of the year.

It's very important to put it on the schedule that those rooms need to be taken care of. They need to be planned. They need to be taken off to schedule and plan on repairing those areas of the hotel or that floor, rather, one at a time or a block of rooms at a time, until those rooms are up to par so you can take them out of your mind and then you can book those rooms without blockage of any type for the busy time period that you're planning.

Christina: What's the best way for a hotel property manager to take this step in terms of really thinking about what is their goal? What's the best way for them to do that?

Orlando: Once a property manager has been sold on the benefits of the improvement, the morale and attitude of the staff will go a long way to accommodate and facilitate the many issues that will arise during the renovation process.

People – the hotel's staff – have to be sold on the idea that this is going to work. Once the attitude and the morale is there, then they're going to say, "Well, sure have them come down, let's fix the rooms." We're going to have a better time doing it at the same time, because we're going to feel like welcomed guests to the hotel staff instead of pests. We want to be able to work with this facility manager and the personnel, at the same time, like where we're welcome there.

Once the goal of achieving clean and beautiful rooms is sold to the people that make the decisions and working in a hotel on a daily basis, everybody is going to be happier so we can accomplish the project on a timely base. You need to be sold on the idea that this is good for them.

Five Key Goals

Christina: Excellent. Tell me a little bit more, I know that sometimes you talk about project management 101, like the five goals every project manager should achieve to aspire. Tell me a little bit about that.

Orlando:
- Completing projects on time,
- Completing projects on budget,
- Meet the requirements,
- Keeping project stakeholders happy,
- Keeping staff happy.

...are among the five most important goals project managers should hold themselves to.

The project manager needs to control every aspect of the project they oversee, from resources and suppliers to project costs and equipment also, it's like staying on top of everything is focus on the five most important goals associated with project management.

If you can meet the following five types of goals for each project, you will achieve project and professional success. Like goal #1, (finish on time), and goal #2, (it should be finished under budget.) Those are the most important ones, but also goal #3 (meet the requirements that will satisfy your project).

Also keep your customers happy. It's important if you still have customers while the renovation is going on. Also goal five is, keep the team members happy, like I said before, people have to be happy that we are doing this project for them, not only for the customers it's also for the people that work in the building; the housekeepers, the cooks, the people in the kitchen, management. Everybody moves around the building during the renovation, and if those people aren't happy and they hate it because too much noise, too much commotion, it's like the attitude and the morale spreads and people go and start hating what's going on. If people are not happy, things don't work very well.

Christina: If employees aren't happy, then your customers – your guests – certainly aren't going to be happy either.

Orlando: Right. They can see that, they can sense that.

Christina: If someone gets stuck on this step, how do they get unstuck?

Orlando: You've heard the five goals above: what needs to be managed and tracked. Simple projects, like a few hours, and even a few days can be managed with a manual system. Online tools are readily available for more lengthy and complicated projects. However, a construction management firm should be consulted for large scale renovations.

Step 3: Cost Containment
Christina: When you think about bathroom renovations, these are expensive investments for hotels and property managers. I imagine this is the phase where a property manager or an operations manager starts looking at ways to contain the cost of a renovation.

In your experience, what are the best questions an operations or property manager should ask, whether it's questions they share themselves or their internal team, or their vendors, what's the best questions they should be asking?

Orlando: They should think with the goal in mind, like I said before. They should walk backwards from there, get their priorities in line: the "needs to have" and the "want to haves."

Then secure estimates, to answer questions like, "How much is it going to cost and how long is it going to take?" Also very important, who is going to do what and when?

Christina: I imagine another one too, I was just thinking about this because when I've worked with vendors in the past, it's important to know the very last detail of what you just said: who's going to do what and when. If somebody doesn't do their job, how does that affect the next party doing their piece of the puzzle as well? Really understanding those roles is really important.

Orlando: That's important because a lot of renovations that managers take on, there is not just one vendor who is the only one involved. Occasionally there are more vendors at the same time, so who's going to do what? And when? It might interfere with the other group of vendors that are coming right after you or before you.

It's important to have a plan of action, especially when you're doing more than just a simple renovation. If you're doing carpeting for instance, if you're doing furniture, if you're doing painting, these things need to be organized in a timely manner and there needs to be a schedule that needs to be put on the calendar, when is it going to start, who's going to come in next, who's going to come before. Everything has to be organized in a timely manner preferably on a schedule on a computer if it allows, but somebody has to take the responsibility to manage these on a timely manner and orderly manner.

Understanding Refinishing: What is it? Is It Right for Your Renovation?

Christina: One of the ways a hotel or property manager can contain the cost of a bathroom renovation is through refinishing. Orlando, help me understand ... because I've heard a lot of terms thrown around. What is refinishing – or resurfacing – what is that?

Orlando: I'm going to try to make it clear for you. Refinishing or resurfacing, and or re-glazing are genuine trades that require training, practice as well as expert personal craftsmanship. It's spraying fixtures or tile walls with a coating to make it look nicer, newer-looking, be waterproof, to make it look like new. That's basically in a nutshell what that is.

Christina: Is that the same as re-glazing?

Orlando: Yes, it's the same. The term has been used interchangeably over the years, but re-glazing it's not really the appropriate term.

Re-glazing implies that you're going to put the glaze back in the fixture which -- unless you have an oven capable of 2300 degrees.... That's not what you're doing.

We are refinishing and putting the life back onto the existing finish... we're not putting new porcelain on the finish. Nobody can say that, if they're telling you that, they're not telling the truth.

Christina: What can be refinished or resurfaced?

Orlando: Basically everything in the bathroom can be done: bathtubs, sinks, ceramic tiles, counter tops, and other surfaces are resurfaced right in place.

Bathtub refinishing or bathtub re-glazing and refinishing leaves the fixtures with a dazzling new look that is easy to maintain. [It] creates the strongest bond available for a long lasting and beautiful finish with economical and effective bathroom remodeling-like results.

Christina: Why is it such a cost saver?

Orlando: It saves money and time. The high cost of labor to tear down a bathroom, plus new labor to install all new fixtures, and the added materials is the main reason why refinishing has been such a popular option for project managers especially for commercial and hospitality clients, which must maintain these apartments units on a regular base.

Christina: How else can this approach be a benefit to the property manager or the operations manager. Such as, it can be cost savings, for your rooms to be closed off, less of a hitch of revenue, what are other benefits?

Orlando: All of the above. Cost savings [by doing refinishing or resurfacing] are about 75% of actual full remodeling. That's not unusual. And then you can actually get this done for a quarter of the cost that would take you to rip out everything and do everything new. Also, [refinishing allows for] same day turnaround [which allows] for all the trades to work on the room.

Like I said before, some renovations involve all the trades, so when you do refinishing, you can do everything in one day and you're out of the room for the next trade to come in and do something else. You get faster completion, faster delivery, and faster results.

Case Studies: Four Points Sheraton and The W Hotel

Christina: Wow, I didn't know that. Is there one particular story or case study or an example that you'd like to share that could really sum up what we've been talking about here?

Orlando: Yes. Back in late 2014, and last year, '15, we completed two Four Points Hotels by Sheraton hotels here in Manhattan. Management was pressed for time, the holidays were right upon them and 30 days away, and the hotel was selling out quickly. We set out to refinish all 135 room showers like new. Every room, the floor was done each day, with 24-hour turnaround and they were ready to use the same day basically, saving them months of delay. You can imagine all the [potential] discomfort unhappy guests. And the best part was about $240,000 worth of savings compared to new remodeling.

Christina: Wow, $240,000 is not a small amount of money.

Orlando: Now, imagine what you can do in a hotel with that much money. You can do a lot of carpeting, or a lot of furniture with that.

Christina: Yeah, exactly. You said that there was another example that you had of a debut hotel as well.

Orlando: Yes. Also a good-sized general contractor: we helped them save money renovating the W Hotel in Lexington Avenue [Manhattan, New York]. We were hired to refinish all 110 bathtubs. Again, they were pressed for time and budget issues. They relied on us to deliver the result he needed. They were very happy after that.

Christina: That's fabulous, that you can turn a project around in such a way and under budget in such a way that you're not impacting a hotel's big travel time or at the holidays et cetera, that's amazing.

Orlando: Not at all. We can run in there, actually almost unnoticed by other trades, kind of work behind the scenes, get our stuff done and before, let's say we can work on a weekend, because a lot of times we've been asked to do that. Work in a weekend Saturday and Sunday sometimes. Of course, it takes more money to do that, but we can do it. We can do a Saturday or Sunday installation, and do a lot of rooms and before the people and other trades come back to the remodeling task on Monday morning, and everything [on our end] is done.

Pro Tips for Running a Successful Renovation

Christina: What are the big opportunities in bathroom renovation that many beginners or even maybe some experienced property manager, owners, or operations managers, what are they possibly missing?

Orlando: Let's see, most managers don't know that we're able to offer a combination of things. These can really make a difference in their bottom line. Let me explain that.

By taking advantage of the options available like refinishing and re-glazing, that we talked about, we can clearly see what the impact on the bottom line would be and what effect of saving time would have on occupancy rates.

What managers are not aware of is that, they can actually take a step further because of these achievable savings. Managers can get more back for the renovation dollars and introduce new flooring and new fixtures, new high quality acrylic bathtubs, and shower liners as an alternative to refinishing without going to extremes. They can get great results that will amaze, save a lot of resources in the process and achieve their ultimate goal of customer satisfaction.

Time and time again, we have helped managers with a complete upgrade including refinishing bathtubs, showers, wall tile refinishing, vanity sinks and new flooring, using attractive porcelain, marble, or granite tile with amazing results.

Christina: Are there any other steps at this point that a property manager or an owner or an operations manager should know about when getting started thinking about renovations and how to contain those costs?

Orlando: Sure.

Pick the right contractor to do the job.

They have to think of picking the right contractor to do the job. [That's] very important. Experience in hotel and industrial applications is a must. Manpower and equipment are also a concern. They must be able to provide enough personnel to work on 10 or 20 rooms per floor (if that's what the job is requiring).

Most hotel bathrooms have no windows, or windows that don't opening wide enough for venting equipment. [So the contractor will need to provide good venting equipment.] The right venting is very important, and needs to be provided or the smell will travel, make people uncomfortable, and guests will be looking elsewhere the next time around.

I've heard dozens of stories about other competitors using faulty venting equipment, or no venting at all. [I've seen them leave] dust on furniture, over spray, masking materials and waste behind, and worse of all, I've heard of a time that an actual guest came out of the room to complain to the workers about the smell in the hallways. Not a good scenario to say the least.

With our 30 years working in hotels in New York City, we know what it takes to handle these projects. We're very familiar with hotel environments, engineering and housekeeping personnel. We never underestimate the reason [for us being there]: we're there to save you time and money.

Select the right bathtub refinishing coating.

They need to select the right bathtub refinishing coating, bathtub refinishing in commercial locations is a much different job than residential installations. First, there is venting issues. Venting is a must regardless of what people may tell you, the right bathtub refinishing process is also very important.

If the coating is to last any longer than a year, you better make sure you're getting a high quality professional acrylic urethane enamel coating.

There are versions that claim to have very little smell and dry within hours. Those are called "wonder products." But the reality is, a good coating would have reduced VOCs. That's volatile organic compounds, the number that most of our engineers are aware of and legally it has to be within the range of numbers allowed by law, but they all smell.

Select the right bathtub refinishing process.
I have been refinishing bathtubs for over 30 years, I tried most of the products available and never have been convinced enough about bathtub refinishing systems that do not use an acid etching process, don't use a primer system to ensure bonding and relies solely on a low quality fast dry coating. I support the tried and true method of throughout cleaning, caulking removal, acid etching and epoxy primer, followed by the best quality aliphatic acrylic urethane system. It is really the only way to get guaranteed consistent good results.

Make sure to include the right value added services.
Also, the added value services is what do you get with that. The right bathtub refinishing job is not complete without these essential services.

- Clean-up after completion for instance: tape and paper removal should not be left to housekeeping or engineering to be removed. It should be removed by the refinisher after completion.

- Nonslip finish should be included in this scope of work as a safety measure not as an option. Falls in tubs and showers are still the number one reason for hotel lawsuits by guests. Don't be a statistic, you need to request that and make sure it's in the paperwork that you're getting.

- A professional silicone caulking line around the tub or showers is a must for a professional installation. We talked about that before, not a task for engineering or staff, they're not experienced or trained to do that but unfortunately, it's a very often overlooked area of the bathrooms in a lot of properties I have seen over the years.

We are proud, to have been told hundreds of times that we deliver a professional looking caulking line.

Choose people you can trust.
Work with people that you can trust, is another essential thing that you need to have. It's always one of the most important things to consider, today, in these tough economic times, contractors come and go. A lot of people can sell you promises they cannot keep, and put your reputation at risk.

Does that answer your question?

Christina: I think it does. To boil that down, your best advice, your best tips [for the renovation process] are to:

- pick the right contractor for the job,

- select the right bathtub refinishing coating,

- select the right bathtub refinishing process,

- make sure about those added value services, there's no such thing as not enough safety in the world, we need to make sure that the bathroom is safe, and

- always work with people you can trust.

Those are really, really good pieces of advice. Is there anything else?

Orlando: I believe they go together, not only for this type of project, but for everything that you attempt to do. You have all these basic needs ... They're achievable but believe it or not, a lot of people don't ask for these things or they don't make sure they're put in writing.

Christina: Or that they don't know, exactly.

Orlando: True.

Christina: That's great advice. Is there anything else I haven't asked or about getting started with the formal bathroom renovation that you'd like to share with our audience, the property managers, owners or operations managers?

Orlando: Yes. The handy old cliché, KISS, you remember that Christina?

Christina: I sure do.

Orlando: It's "keep it short and simple." You make sure you do what needs to be done, it's done on time, on budget and everyone is happy. I think that sums it all up, I mean, what else is there, if you can get all those goals right there where they need to be, I think you're in good company.

Christina: I couldn't agree more. Thank you so much Orlando Salazar for a great interview and I'm sure all the property managers, and owners, and operations managers in our audience have a much clearer understanding of getting started with affordable bathroom renovation, now that you've laid everything else so clearly. Thank you so very much for sharing your expertise and your experiences so graciously today.

Can you tell us a bit more about hoteltubspro.com, specifically how does it help beginner property managers, owners or operations managers with how to get the luxury bathrooms you want at a fraction of the cost and half the time?

Orlando: Sure, I can do that, yes. The best part of our solution is that we offer a 100% risk free trial of our service so there is no risk. Your satisfaction is assured through our no risk, you can't lose, a 100%, no questions asked, money back guarantee.

Before they embark in a bathroom refinishing multi unit project, they can visit our website which is hoteltubspro.com, or they can call our toll free line 1-877-882-3621. They can have us do it sample at our regular fee, if for any reason, they're not thrilled or satisfied with our refinishing sample, just contact me directly within 30 days, and we'll refund a 100% of your purchase price. There are no hard feelings.

Christina: Thank you again, Orlando P. Salazar, for sharing with us today, and thank you all the property managers, and owners, and operations managers in our audience for joining us for this amazing beginners guide presentation about affordable bathroom renovation, to help you get off on the right start.

Orlando: Thank you, Christina.

Christina: Again I'm Christina McCale and thanks again for joining us on revitalizing your bathrooms. I'd like to invite you to join us at the hoteltubspro.com today for more on how you can succeed with affordable bathtub renovations and affordably remodeling bathrooms and refinishing or resurfacing. Thanks so very much!

Get Future Updates!

Want to take this interview with you?

Be sure to visit our website at hoteltubspro.com
Where you can join our email list to be notified
of future pro tips, e-books and guides for hotel renovation.

And get the audio of this interview free!

Just sign up here.